Th

When your feet won't move,
Let the winds of words carry you

By:
David B. Rossman

Forewords by:
Fiona Reeves and Steven P. Miskimens

The Journey
When your feet won't move,
Let the winds of words carry you

Poetry Books three and four combined

Book Three
WE SHALL BE HIS
Write it on my heart

Book Four
In His Time
With every beat of a poem, He knows my heart

Printed in the United States by Morris Publishing
3212 East Highway 30
Kearney, NE 68847
1-800-650-7888

Copyright

The Journey
When your feet won't move,
Let the winds of words carry you

Poetry Books Three and Four combined

© 1998 By: David B. Rossman
Printed in 2003

ISBN: 0-9718475-1-7
LOCC: 2003094008

Manufactured in the United States
10 9 8 7 6 5 4 3 2 1

DAVID B. ROSSMAN
PO Box 2072
Yelm, WA 98597-2072

Acknowledgements

Father God
I thank Thee
For sending your
Holy Spirit
To flow through me

Since this book was written under the influence of the Holy Spirit I feel it is only fitting to acknowledge that without Jesus, this book would not have been written.

With each new poem written I felt closer to Him. His powerful loving arms held me as He unleashed the Holy Spirit within me.

I have never felt so close to Christ, but I know that the intimacy between us has yet to happen in the fullness in which it is meant to be.

Dedication

My family and my friends.

Thanks to Abe Cleary for the pictures on
both covers. You've captured the moments
of thought and of joy.

Fiona Reeves for the kind words and
encouragement shared.

Be blessed everyone.

Special Thanks To

God the Father and His Son, Jesus
For the gift of writing and the guidance in
which to do it.

My wife, Donna
For loving me enough to let me chase after
the dream.

Joshua, William and Anita Rose
For the love and inspiration you three have
placed within this father's heart.   Be
forever blessed and loved.

Janine
I've seen you write and heard you sing.
You are a true blessing.

Steve Miskimens
You are gifted beyond compare.   Thanks for
the friendship and the chance to see poetry
through another's eyes.

Dan, Norma and Les
ASSIST Ministries
For your continued support and prayers

Book Three

WE SHALL BE HIS
Write it on my heart
The Poetry Continues

Foreword

I have found that at certain turning points in my life, God has sent special people into my life to help me see the light. David Rossman is just such a person.

Despite a physical encumbrance that would have overcome many, David accepts his disability as God's will, inspiring all who come in to contact with him. For every cloud, there is a silver lining. David, through his pain and suffering, shows all of us that dedicating ourselves to God makes every challenge meaningful.

As his emotions flow onto paper in the form of poignant poetry, David Rossman becomes a strong and whole man sharing with us a very special gift given to him by his Lord and Savior.

Thank you David for your warm smile, your wonderful outlook on life and your inspiring words. You have helped me make an important change in my life.

--Fiona Reeves
Formerly of Nisqually Valley News

BOOK THREE

TABLE OF CONTENTS

A Moment Of Silence

God comes down upon us
As we hold each other's hand
He reaches out
To lift us up
And walk across the land
Without a word
He lets us know
That we are all He needs
He asks us to
Be spreading His word
And planting up new seeds
As we listen to His voice
He whispers in our ear
And says how much He loves us
And that He is always near
So take the time
To stop and listen
And hear the words
He may say
And you will know
The time is right
To take the time to pray

A Prayer For His Parents

Dear Lord Jesus
This I pray
Let them feel this
Right away
This is hard
For them I know
To watch and see
Their son go
But it is of you
So he must follow
Be with them
As he leaves
Let it be Your Light
He sees
I know at times
Things don't seem fair
But use this as a testimony
To show them you are there

A Price Paid

There is a price to pay
To live the Christian way
No road is always smooth
There's always a bend
A groove
Taking the hand of God
Gives evenness to odd
Persecution rocks the boat
When Jesus tries
To keep us afloat
Putting on the Armor
And taking the sword
The victory is won
Great is our reward
"I love You, Lord
Walk with me
Talk with me
Keep me from going down there"
Is more than a prayer
It's an oath signed in faith
Faith gives you power to stand
To give Christ a hand
Remember reading about it?
The price was paid
When He walked this land

Angel On Earth

Angel? O sweet Angel
Sent from up above
To be by the side
Of her one true love
Jesus gave His life
So the two of you would see
How much He loves you
And get you close, you see?
A lifetime shared
With the man you stand beside
Jesus will reveal the deep love
You may hide
A rainbow above
To show Him promise
The snow falls
To show purity and newness
A heart beat for God
A man and her son
Without you there
What would get done?
A husband who knows
You love him so
But sits in front of the 'puter
'Til he glows
Through it all your love shall never fall
Thank You Jesus
For an Angel right here on earth

Another Long Night

Again I'll say
I'm glad you're alright
I waited by the phone
You may have called
It's gonna be
Another long night
Ready for some poetry?
It still hurts
That you are there
If you could call
We could share
There are things inside
I need to let out
We are brother
Is there any doubt?
God has a plan
Though Satan threw a curve
Let's get back on track
Giving our weakest link
Its strength back
Come on, Bro,
Give me a call
I promise you
I won't let you fall

Be Strong And Of Good Courage

There will be a time
When all you feel
Seems wrong
But remember
I have been with you
All along
You fight the battle
Between Good and evil
Darkness and Light
Just know that in the end
All will be right
Your hearts beat
With the same rhythm and rhyme
Because your two hearts
Are the same as mine
To love each other
As you do
Is only because I asked you to
Be strong and of good courage
Let nothing you dismay
For the bond and love
You two have
Is a brother and Godly love
That will NEVER fade away
I give you my WORD!

- JESUS -

Broken Hearted

You were told by God
To do what was right
I began to sleep better
At night
We talked day in
And we talked day out
Words from our hearts
Were spoken
There is no doubt
Satan showed you
But you wouldn't listen
I tested and tried
To push you away
Here you said
You would always stay
But now I know
The extent Satan will go
Just listening to the talk
Of passes and snow
Tears now fall
From my eyes
Now on the chopping block
My heart lies.

I Can't Fight This Feeling

Fight it? Do I dare?
A passion for Him
I know is there
I can feel it
Building from within
Wanting to know Him
Is to desire Him
Caring for Him
Is to hear with my heart
All that He has to say
Standing firm
Not turning away
When I asked for the courage
To stay strong
He knows where I belong
Seeking His face
Seeing in His eyes
A passion we share
Thank you Lord Jesus,
I know that You care
'Cause I can't fight this feeling

Clear Future

In the days ahead
Your past will be shed
All will be clear
Live by faith
Not by fear
Believe in all
That I have foretold
Stay firm
Stand bold
Promises given
By my word alone
Your future
Will then be shown
It may take time
Wait and see
Pray for the spirit
Walk with Me
I will not break the promise
I gave thee
Sleep easy
And worry free
Your future lies
With Me

Could You Love Me Any More

Your gentle voice
Melts me from within
Down on my knees
I pray and speak Your name
Could You love me any more?
Pops into mind
I know the answer
In my heart
It's in Your Word
That's where I'll start
I look up
With tears in my eyes
And see Your grim
Shine down from the skies
Could You love me any more?
Let Your Spirit
Send me to the floor
Could I love You any more?

Deep Cleaning

Deep inside
Darkness lives
Secret lies
Little fibs
Running rampant
Churning our souls
Satan tries
To meet his goals
One less for Christ
One more for me
Jesus sits and smiles
For He knows His time will come
When it comes to the battle
Jesus will have won
Go ahead Satan, you will imp
I'll wait...then dig dig dig
Deep within the cleaning will start
Starting with your heart
The pain you feel
The things you hide
Will let you go
If in someone you will confide
Me...Trust in Me
I love you
You'll see
Let me in
And I'll clean you out

Fired Up

From my feet
To my knees
I will fight
I won't retreat
Satan's threats
Will not land
For on the Bible
I will stand
From deep within
I feel the burn
Flames are rushing
To the surface
Charring all the pain
Satan's loss
Is Christ's gain
I will survive
All that comes about
Christ is my rock
The Bible
My two edged sword
I am on fire
For the Lord

First Snow

First snow of the year
Beautiful but dangerous
I fear
The clouds have fallen
To earth just this morn'
I wonder when the first
Snowman will be born
Today is the day
They said would never come
But who is in control?
The weathermen
Or God, the Might One?
The latter of the two
It would be safe to say
For everyone's safety
This I pray
On this January 11, 1998
Cook brisk white day

Follow Your Heart

I had a feeling
About today
I waited for you
But there was little to say
When the phone rang
This evening instead
The foreseen outcome
Was in my head
To hear you cry
Fighting the battle inside
Made me see
How much you mean to me
I know in my heart
God will bring you here
But Satan got to you
While you were still there
Now you're gone
Though the direction
I don't know
Follow your heart and His
And when we meet once again
We shall sing praises of glory
And begin a new start

From Friends To Brothers

From the first word typed
Across the screen
I knew more than friends
We would be
Brothers we became
To that Jesus
Has seen
We stepped before Him
He pulled ahead
Not now
Not yet
In My time
The answer to prayer
You will get
Listening to Him
Has been a reward
Blessings abound
As we wait
For His timing
To come around

Give Me Reassurance

As the hours pass
And the sun rises
I can't help
But wipe the tears from my eyes
I try to stay positive
And think that all is okay
But has the bond
Gone away?
I pray for reassurance
To know that he's just fine
He's a friend
And a brother
With You in mind
Are we drifting further apart?
I feel the pain beating
Does he feel it
In his heart?
Dear God
I ask this in Jesus' name
Give me reassurance
Please, just the same

Given By Your Heart

Show me visions
Of times to come true
Make an impression
Help me follow You
Tell me what
You want me to do
I need to know
Where ever You lead
I will go
If there is a time
Or a need to take care of
You will do it
With Your unending love
Learning of salvation
Is a lesson to take
Putting You first
And the rest
You will make
Loving You
With all my heart
Trusting in faith
You won't take back
Your promises
Given from your heart

Glorious Grace

At the base
Of the cross I fell
Seeking His face
To fill this empty shell
I cried and pleaded
Pour Your grace
Upon me Father
The pain I felt
Would not let me be
Then I sought
His blood on me
Drip by drip—drop by drop
The pain slipped
The hurting stopped
Looking up
His feet inches
From my eyes
I saw the blood
Gush from His side
I smiled with joy
As I was submerged
In this Holy Spirit flood
Yes Lord
Give me your glorious grace
Cleanse me when I seek your face
Purify me
Before I leave this place

Greetings

Greetings is the name
Jesus is no game
There are no losers
All will win
If you turn
Away from sin
He talks of love
And wants to share
Smile when He speaks to you
His greetings are always there

Guard Down - Wall Up

Satan got you
On the run
Off the path
Shown by the Son
And though you swore
This wouldn't happen
It has
Yes I was firm
The last we talked
But my wall has gone up
Since your guard went down
Now everyone notices
I wear a frown
I can still hear your tear
Over the phone
My eyes feel like a river
The tears have flowed
I can't help
But think of you
Every minute of the day
And wonder how
Satan pulled you away

What did I do wrong?

He Gave Me Reassurance

The call
An answer to prayer
Thank You Jesus
Your voice
Soothing to
My heart
A peace
He gave me reassurance
This is confirmation
To the fact
He is in control
I have to wait
Now and see
How long it will be
I trust in Him though
He knows
What's right
For you and I
Now I won't
Have to cry
Satan's hold
Has been torn
Yours voice
Has released that thorn

He Has My Attention

He has my attention
That I see
The snow flurries started
At 3:30 this morning
By this afternoon
There should be snow warning
Fluffy and white
It glides in my sight
What was boring at Christmas
Is now covered in white
Is upstate New York
Friends fight the ice
If they could come visit
That would be nice
Although it is snowing now
A trip that once was
Thought to be fun
May only be dangerous now
We still have our power
And thank God that we do
With none it would be hard
'Cause we'd be outta heat too
"Dear God keep us safe…
With power and all
Keep everyone safe
As the snow does fall"

Hear Him Calling

The walls are dull
And boring too
Listen...
Hear Him calling you?
Use this time
To get priorities straight
If nothing else
Read the Word
Build your faith
I sat by the phone
After it went dead
Thousands of thoughts
Went through my head
"God," I said
"Keep them safe
Keep them fed.
I wish, Father God,
There was more I could do."
"Stay calm and diligent in prayer
Trust that I will take care
Of them for you."
One day we shall see
A testimony shared
Between families

Heart To Heart

We talked of walks
In the rain
And of wanting
Only God's gain
To see His glory
In our lives
We may have to suffer
Unwanted pain
We talked with our hearts
All of the time
I'd do all I can for you
At the drop of a dime
We talked of mountain streams
Godly visions
And vivid dreams
God has a plan
His Grace keeps away
Satan's schemes
The walk in the rain
Was the last before it was first
But for God
We still thirst
One day we shall see
The pain in our hearts
Set free
If only now
You could talk to me

Heavenly Dreams

Heavenly dreams?
Yes, you see
Clouds and laughter
In the now and hereafter
Warmth of knowledge
A peace… a grace
Silent happiness upon
His face

Heavenly dreams?
Yes, you see
Visions of the yet to come
Where He leads
I will follow
Having Father and son
Talks with Him
Thank you Father
For the ear that listens
And the hand that does not let go

Heavenly dreams?
Yes, you see
Him on the wood
Me beneath…Crying out
"Lord, if only I could…"

Blood drips from above
His undying love
Landing in my hand
Clearer now
It's plain to see
Sin has been washed
Away from me

Heavenly dreams?
Yes, you'll see
Life with the Father
Has trial and persecution
Yes indeed
But life without
The Father
Means death
For certain

Heavenly dreams?
Yes, you see
The reason why
He set us free

Heavenly dreams?
Yes, you'll understand
Close your eyes
Ask and confess
Pray for the vision
Share in these heavenly dreams

Heaven's Heartbeat

Be a servant to Me
A husband
A daddy
Love your family
Quit playing games
With your heart
Heaven's heartbeat
Is what counts
Listen to it
Hear it's gentle rhythm
Heaven's heartbeat
It's clean and clear
No confusion there
Do the right thing
Say no to the wrong
If you don't
You're just pulling Me along
Turn from sin
Be a servant
Your whole life long
Heaven's heartbeat
Is in the clouds
Colors of the sunrise
Shimmer of sunset on the water
Be true to Heaven's heartbeat
And I'll be true to you

His Last Stand

I knelt beneath Him
My head bowed
My face in hands
I felt His blood drip, washing me
The nails
The thorns
The plea
His last stand
How could He free a world
He could have freed Himself?
That answer only God knows
His eyes closed
His face streaked with red
How painful it must have been

If the wages of our sins
Caused His death—
How painful will it be for those
Who don't believe?

His Will In You

When I see your picture
I see His will in you
Your love for him
Grows stronger
With everything
That you do
Your smile
Shows His glory
In your voice
I hear His music
There is a peace within
I can see it
Under your skin
Your eyes are windows
To your soul
His will in you
Wherever you go

Hit Your Knees

When the storm rolls in
Darkness and clouds galore
Get out of the water
Head for the shore
If on land
When destruction falls
His your knees
Give out the calls
Demons rush in
Power and evil
Demanding surrender
Fight back
Don't give any slack
Pray in earnest
Constant and headlong
Seek the face
Of the Righteous one
To Him be the glory
His be the victory
Storms will calm
Pray with a sweaty palm
With perspiration on your face
Stay on your knees
That's the place
Fight like a man of God
Praying one for all
And all for One

Holy Ghost Covering

My heart longs
To learn
For Christ
I want the fire
To burn
Serving Him
The best I can
Means being patient
Wanting in His time
Holy Ghost power
I have felt
Satan's hold
Began to melt
Holy Ghost coverage
As I prayed
Hands on family-I laid
Blow up their noses
I was told
See Me work
As you stand bold
Laughter broke loose
Anger gone
With Holy Ghost coverage
Jesus has won

HOME

The streets are paved
With brilliant gold
Not like those
Of my earthly home
The sound soars
Of an angel choir
Not of gloom
Destruction and evil power
I'll walk now
Where I once was carried
I now live
Empty is the place
Where I was buried
New legs I have
No longer do I stumble
But a lesson
Taught on earth
Fight, don't dwell and struggle
I like this place
Heaven called home
It sure beats earths
Astroturf and Styrofoam

I Can't Find The Words

We took to each other
So fast
Our words deeply felt
I couldn't believe
Our heart connected
I warned you this may happen
But you weren't going to let it
Get in the way
God was leading
This we prayed
My heart leaped
When you said
You were coming
Now it's on the table
And tears are on the floor
God, I pray
You walk through my door
Until then
I can't find the words

I Loved You Once

I loved You once
For the feelings I felt
Whenever Your name
Came up in conversation
Or the words said
When we spoke
My head reeled
My heart tugged
My feelings became unplugged
I love You more today
Why I cannot say
There's more I have to say
I just have to find the way
If I never get the chance
Or even get to see You
At a glance
I want You to know
I loved You once
But I love you more today

I Want To Be In Love With You

I think of You
My heart races
Tears fill my eyes
At the image of Your face
I battle enemies
I plead the blood
Of the Lamb
Take me Father
Show me home
Clothe me in white
And wings
Take away all my earthly things
I know You love me Father
Without a doubt this it true
Lord
I want to be in love with You

I Remember

When Christ died
At Calvary
I read that the price
Was paid for me
When He rose
On the third day
Salvation was mine
I have to say
The pain He felt
Though the process was hart
Was taken away with the sin
Of the world's bad start
We won the victory
When you read me
That poem you wrote
I couldn't help
But cry inside
Feeling the lump in my throat
Your words came across
So loud so clear
I believed them then
All to be true
Now the worse I fear
Come on my brother
What do I do?

I've Seen The Proof

I'VE SEEN THE PROOF
Proof of what?
His grace
His presence
The joy praise brings

I'VE SEEN THE PROOF
Proof of what?
His love that is never ending
His promises kept
His guidance to pull me through

I'VE SEEN THE PROOF
Proof of what?
His loving honesty
His rejoicing in forgiveness
His warmth in caring

I'VE SEEN THE PROOF
Proof of what?
His protection during persecution
His victory over sin
His answer to prayer

I'VE SEEN THE PROOF
Proof of what?
All this and more
How, when and where, you ask?
Faith, everyday, everywhere
Where's the proof of all this, you ask?
The Bible—
Just ask and He will show you the proof

In A Flash

In the moment
That we sin
We have to start
All over again
It's scary at first
But it could be worse
Take that step
You won't regret
Hit your knees
And ask for forgiveness
Please
In a flash
It may all be done
Will you be gone?
Like a thief
The grave He will rob
If you are ready
Your heart will throb
Going...going...gone
It will seem
Then poof
In a flash
It's no dream
Are you ready?
It's the rapture

In Love All Over Again

We stood at opposite sides
Of the rainbow
At the start
Each praying for
The other's heart
Now, three months shy
Of three years later
She makes my heart pound
Off its indicator
When times came about
When we felt unloved
That's when His love
Came from above
I love her
And need her
So very much
I want the best for her
The best health for her
She makes me tingle
With her touch
A hug here—a flower there
A beautiful daughter we share
Her eyes say she loves me
That I cannot deny
But for the life of my
I don't know why

In The Distance

When we talk
It strengthens my walk
The bond of brotherhood
Is there
Christ's love we share
In the distance though
A snag waits
It's the pull between
Hell and Heaven's gates
If there is no communication
The snag gets nearer
That is what I mostly fear
I try to think positive thoughts
For that is what
God would do
It hurts not to talk
Each day that passes
It weakens my walk
I understand my responsibilities
I know that I am to do
But in the distance
I still miss you

It's Never Too Late!

It's never too late to give Him your heart.
It's never too late to do your part.

It's never too late for love
It's never too late as long as it's from
above.

It's never too late to be a friend.
It's never too late to hold their hand.

It's never too late to see or hear.
It's never too late to let Him wipe that
tear.

Just Give Jesus Your Heart
It's Never Too Late.

Whispers Of The Heart

Either in the deepest valley
Or the tops of a mountain
Christ should find us
On our knees

We thing
He doesn't care
Good times
Bad times
With us all
These He shares

Listen closely for His voice
Be sensitive to His touch
He sees every step
Hears every whisper
Not just from the mouth
But also from the heart

Judas' Kiss

It must be tough
Being Lord of all
Crying when someone
Doesn't answer Your call
You hear all the time
People will follow
Only if certain things
You allow
Shall they turn You over
To the high priest
Thirty pieces of silver
At least
There is a man
Further down the road
He said he loved You
So You were told
Satan took hold
When his guard was down
Turn the cheek
A kiss will be found
Tears fall
When Judas' kiss
Sounds the call

Just To See You Smile

Today I tried
To think things through
But all I thought about
Was you
God has a plan
For you I know
Follow Him
Where He tells you to go
I know that it hurts
I feel the pain inside
I've done nothing
But wonder why
Then hide my face and cry
I would do anything
To see your smile
Another mile
My brother
I know you feel this too
When you get here
I'll be here for you

Just Watching

Here on earth we stand
Lost children
In a vast land
Wondering where
We belong
Looking for
The Father all along
Some turn away
Some come to stay
He wants us
In His house
To play games and study
Learning from His word
Not worrying of money
He will be with you
From the start
You know that
In your heart
Your salvation was bought
On the cross years ago
Just how much He loves you
Ask and He will show
He is up there
Just watching
Over us
Knowing what we'll say
Who we will trust
He is a great God
The Might One
So...
If you're on the sidelines
Just watching for fun
Jesus really loves you
There's no need to run

Killing My Old Man

I saw what they did to You
The nails
The spear
The blood
The pain
What was there to gain?
You gave up Your live
You hung there for me
My old ways keep coming back
It is strength I lack
When my flesh is weak
You become my strength
Place him there
My old man
Put him on the tree
Yes, I see
The nails
The blood
The pain
What is there to gain?
Freedom in Christ, my Lord
This is true
Father, help me to live for You
Instead of for the old man
That I once knew

Letting Go

Now that I've heard your voice
I have no other choice
But to let you go
In my mind...
That is
What has to be done
Don't tell it
To my heart
It will deny it
From the start
Letting go
Is not easy at all
I sit by the phone
And wait for the call
 I like to heart
The happy sound of your voice
But I really
Have no other choice
God has to do
What He deems best
Something that will
Work out for you
And in order for
This to be so
I have to say
I'm letting go

Life Without You

Before we met
I was lost
There was a void within
No one could fill
Satan tried to
Cover it with sin
I heard the voice
I thought I'd never hear
There was a time
You were asked
To come here
In spirit You did
But physically
You are there
There is a phone line
Directly to You
If I have need
I know what to do
Pray and dial
A number never busy
Will You always have time
To listen to me?
My life has been changed
For the better I know
Life without You?
Whatever!
NO!

Lift The Shade

The moon is out
The sun is gone
Alone again I fear
I know He is watching
But Satan is again near
Death knocks at one side
Life at the other
Run to the window
Peek through the shade
There is Satan
Why won't he fade?
A voice calls out
I've gone with you before
He spoke
Don't listen to Satan
You'll die for sure
Lift the shade
Hear what I say
Life with Me is never ending
I cried out loud
Please Lord help
Then turn away
Again I heard Him say
Run if you want
But you won't get far
I know where you are
Lift the shade
Smile at me
If you resist him
Satan must flee
Dance and rejoice
Sing praises to Me
Lift the shade
The Son has risen

Little Child Lost

This is a child
You know so well
She wants to serve
Her God All Mighty
It gives her joy
And away from hell
Life for this child
Has not been easy
You know this-You see
Time and again
She wonders "Why?"
Where does she belong?
Can she spread her wings and fly?
Her father isn't around
Her mother cannot be found
She wants a home full of love
And rules from above
This home is too lenient
That one is too strict
She searches for one
Where satan's butt will be kicked
Lord, lead her
To the home that's right
One where her faith will grow
And she won't have to fight

Love Among Brothers

When you called
The other night
My heart was hit
With fright
I heard your tears
And held back mine
My turn for being strong
Was at that time
After you left
And drove away
There was nothing more
That I could say
I cried all night
Just like tonight
There is a love
Between brothers
I know
But a love between
Brothers in Christ
Is not afraid to show
I have to talk
To you alone
We need to build up
What satan has blown

My Heart's Tears

You said to be happy
Smile a lot
The more I heard from you
The happier I got
Satan now
Has pulled you away
Tears are all my heart knows
It has nothing more to say
We prayed
Laughed
And cried a little
With each prayer
Chuckle and tear
The bond was thickening
Never to be severed
Now you've gone another way
Through your tears
I heard you say
You loved me
I couldn't take it
Giving into fears
There's nothing left
But my hearts tears

My Letter Returned

I cried inside
When I saw my writing
The enveloped returned
"Moved" in red
That was all
Nothing else said

I've been where y'all are
I won't force the matter
Courts can hurt kids
And leave me sadder

"Time will heal...
The wounds go away..."
I don't think so

As long as I live
The love, the pain
Within my heart will stay

In God's timing
We will see each other

My Two Friends

Distance can make a mile
A friend can make a smile
God gives love
That can free a child
Lost on earth
Found in Christ
Living like Christians
Not like scared mice
Be it by plane
Or by computer screen
Y'all are the neatest
Friends I've seen
One down under
The other up state
I'm in my office
Typing in "Howdy Mate"
If we never meet on earth
One day in Heaven
We will be
We shall share God's Glory
You and me

New Horizon

Nope...go on and have fun
Don't let Satan
Get you on the run
Turn on him
And state your claim
That Jesus is Lord
And He'll remain the same

Just keep looking up
To the new horizon there
For God has a plan for you
And it is His to share

Now that I've Heard The Words

Now that I've heard the words
To deny it
Would be absurd
Taking them to heart
Would be a great place to start
The power in the tune
Written on the page
Ingrained in my head
With love, not pain
To reject the feelings
For Him
As He has them for me
Is to deny the cross
And the love
He showed for me

O Come On, Be Faithful

The snow's outside
The walls are bleak
This is the time
For His face
You should seek
The Bible is there
Over on the shelf
Read His word
And refresh yourselves
A time to study
A time to bond
His love holds you together
Better than a witch's wand
O come on, be faithful
Trust in Him, you'll see
There is no one trustworthier
Than the One who made
You and me

Of Me

When this trip
Comes about
Without a doubt
That it is...of me
Meditate on the Word
And let my voice
Be heard
Then your heart
Will know
That it is...of me
Trust that I
Have heard your prayers
And know
That it is...of me
Don't ask questions
Or try to step ahead
Just stop and listen
Know that it is...of me

One Steady Heart

There....on the hill
See the three crosses?
On either side
The two thieves
They are dead
The One in the center
Look!
Watch!
He's dead
So you think
He may have
Given up His soul
But He is far from dead
See with your eyes
Feel with your heart
Our hearts beat uneasily
His steady for us
If we ask
We are washed with His blood
Sustained through life
With His heart
Loving and compassionate
Just think
We may still be here on earth
But life as we knew it
Stopped...at the cross

Persecution Sometimes Stinks

Persecution sometimes stinks
Think of how He felt
I get slammed by words
I don't want to hear
Do you think He wanted to be there?
His life was planned
As is ours
His life wasn't easy
Nor is ours
We live through

The persecution and sin
He died because of our suffering
From such as that

Would you trade places with Him...
Knowing that the world rests on your
Shoulders?

Persecution may sometimes stink
But at least we can walk away from it
He couldn't he was stuck...
Do you think?

Power Of Love

I have yet to see You
Face to face
And yet I feel You
With every fiber of my being
Within every hiding place
Father thank You
For loving me so
Please don't ever
Let me go
You embrace my heart
With each loving kind word
You gently speak
My love for You
Gains strength by the minute
Thank You for being strong
When I go weak
I can't help
But see Your face
With my mind's eye
That special tone
Within Your voice
Makes me want to cry
Father thank You
For loving me

Power Outages

Power outages
What do they mean?
God is talking
Time to come clean
Clear out the junk
And the trash as well
Build reinforcements
For the soft shell
Read the Word
Study and pray
Come out from behind that rock
Stand on it and say
"God's greatness will show
Through all this cold snow…"
You may think you'll slip
While on the rock
But God's right there
Just start to talk
Praise and give glory
To the Mighty One
He'll still be there
When all this stuff is done

…the things He'll allow
To get our attention…

"...and being fully convinced that what He
had promised He was also able to perform"
Romans 4:21

Promises Performed

Stepping before the Lord
What a hard way to go
Hearing Him say
His promise is on the way
Should have been enough
My faith failed
It should have been strong
I went ahead of Him
He followed along
I felt that He left me
All to myself
He waited patiently
For me to return
Satan took hold
A lesson I had to learn
He told me once
All I ask
He will give
In His timing
By faith I should live
Running rampant
A carnal mind
Wanting with my heart
Not that of His
His promise
Will come to pass
His promises
Will be performed

Putting Others First

I've always been the one
To see that things get done
To know needs are met
For my family and friends
Is priority yet
For me to take
And not give
Would be the wrong way
For me to live
The things of life
I have been given
For me to ask for more
Would be selfish galore
Things I've said
And really want
Have just passed by
As just a thought
As God does
I shall do
Putting others first
After God
But before me too

Read About The Exchange

See His face?
Feel the Grace?
See His hands?
The holes clear through?
Go on—
See His pierced side?
His feet, the holes, too?
All this He allowed to happen
'Cause He loves you
See the book
The Bible
It is called
Dust-covered stories
Of Christ's youth
His journey
His teachings
His laws
All of it is there
In that Book
Read about the exchange
Have a minute?
Or even two?
Call out His name
On bended knee
And He will gladly
Set you free

Rescue Me?   Rescue You?

Rescue me?
Rescue you?

No leave me here and free yourself

Don't look back
When the time comes
For if I had to choose
You'd be the one
I'd stay behind and watch you go
Only because
I love you so

Riverbank

He worries too much
This is true
"Cause I do the same thing too
Walking on the river bank
Deep in thought
Within sorrow sank
Birds sing in the distance
Music to my ear
Rushing sounds of water
Changing gears
There I sit
And ponder a while
Why are we here?
What is our purpose?
Please Lord, tell me
I want to see the wilderness
I want to smell the pine
Please Lord, take me from
This confusing world of mine
Why is a brotherly love so strong?
We haven't known each other
For very long
Forget I asked that
Lord, I see
If it is from You
It is to be

Ruler

Could be wood-Could be plastic
Or anything at all
Could be hanging
From a nail
On a grocery store wall
Could be string
Or a number line
In a book

Ruler--Let's take another look
He is the One
Who created us all
We were fashioned by His hands
Big or small
He is the King of kings
And Lord of lords
He defeated Satan
When tempted to do wrong
He died at the cross
To make us strong
Ruler of my life
Is Who He is
Not a ruler
Hanging from a nail
This Ruler kept us
From going to hell

Shot Through The Heart

Shot through the heart
And You're to blame
Because of You
I'll never be the same
Your love bought me
Now I am sold
Right through the heart
A burning flame
I'll stand bold
With no shame
Shot through the heart
Into the soul
Salvation for sinners
Is Your goal
Your powerful Holy Spirit
Fills me through and through
All I want
Is to serve You
Down on my knees
I ask You please
Nail me to the tree
Drain me of my blood
Oh Lord God above
I'm shot through the heart
With Your love

Shower Of Blood

If the darkness
Is overwhelming
And there is no end in sight
Think about Him
On that Friday night
You may see death
At the end of the road
Just think of Him
And how He carried
His heavy load
Life gets dumpy for us
This is true
Think of Him
What was He to do?
He died on a cross
To set us free
We cried as we watched
The Savior bleed
Rain fell that night
Covering the tears
His blood flowed down
And still does after all these years
When you take a shower
Or stand in the rain
You may get wet
Do you think it is rain?
Remember the blood...Think again

Sold Out

Knees bent
Head bowed
His blood poured
Submerged in the Spirit
That is what I like
From arm to arm
Head to toenail
There's no way
I'm going to hell
The power of His love
Cleansed me from above
I pray each day
To stay this way
The old me
Is no more
I'm sold out
Living for Jesus
Is my goal
He has saved my soul
If He wants me
To sing and shout
I will because
I am
SOLD OUT

The Dance

Take my hand
Pull me near
The beat of Your heart
I want to hear
A blanket of warmth
Covers me
As the angels
Sing their songs
Of praise and glory
The word You speak
Seem only for me
Gentle yet strong
Never losing meaning
As the tempo changes
Thank You
For loving me enough
To save this dance for me
To do this on earth
Would be freaky to some
But here in heaven
Dancing with You
Only seems
The right thing to do
Looking up
When you say my name
Gives me reassurance
And sets me free

The Father's Child

There he is watching
His child at play
Standing firm on the grass
He watches and laughs
His child runs to him
In his arms he now holds
The child -only three years old
"Daddy," the child said
Holding her mouth
Close to her daddy's head
"Why does Jesus love us so?"
And the down she drops
And off she goes
He wonders
"Yes, Father, why do You love us so?
Why do You do the things You do for us
Even when we don't deserve it?"
Softly and gently the Lord spoke back
"For the same reason
You love that child you see
For as she is your child
So you are Mine!"

The LaLone Family

David is the husband
Angel, his wife
Their son's name is Erik
They want to serve You for life
Father I pray that You're with them today
Give them joy and peace
With each other, please
David is a lowly servant
Much like me
Give him the knowledge of his family
Show them a way to spend time together
And be with You every minute of the day
I am, who knows, how many miles away
I thank You Father for my friends today
Please answer this prayer
With no further delay
Give them each other
Bring them closer today
Give them the desire to read the Word
Even though his Net server is down
I am here and You're always around
We have a blast with the studies
You know
But the bond between family and You
Must be stronger though
Don't take away the friends
You have given to me
But, Lord Father God
Let it be Your printed Words
They see
Thank You Jesus
For the LaLone family

The Look In Your Eyes

You've said
You love me
You've wanted
To reach out
And hug me
Picking me up
And holding me tight
Thank you Father
It feels so right
I've talked of turning away
You said No way
You told me things I know to be true
Because my heart
Believes in You
I renounced my love
For all to hear
The feelings were gone
But You were still near
I write down words
That I know I can
But there will be more
When You take my hand
I can only say so much
In so many tries
The rest will come
From the look in Your eyes

The River Of Life

Deep inside
I feel His love growing
He's giving me a ride
On the river of life
It just keeps flowing
God gave me life - TWICE
Should I love Him
All the more?
Was it my life
He went to the river for?
Or was it my redemption
That He held in store
He lifts me above the rocks
And protects me from the wind
He cleanses me free of sin
With a wave of blood
Pure white
A virgin to love
No more pain
No more Satan's gain
The river of life
Flows ever more
He's knocking at our hearts' door
He'll hold back the worldly flood
And give you His Life's Blood

The Wind Blows On

On a bench
Near the river's edge
I sit
Wondering where
In God's plan
I fit
Bowing my head
Eyes tightly closed
Hands clenched hard
Will my prayer be heard?
The wind blows gently
His voice comes near
He heard the prayer
The praise I'll share
The wind blows on
I turn my head
Following its direction
There a lady
Her child
Two girls
And a brother stand
The wind blows on
There is my plan
In which you fit
Go and be one
With your family

There Are Three Hearts

There are three hearts
Beating as one
A love binds them together
So the Father's will
Is done
One goes before
The other two then follow
Just stand close He will lead the way
To follow Him
Is choice and a feeling
To do the right thing
Is always more appealing
Walk the waves
Withstand the flames
Bust the falling rock
He will protect and give comfort
To His flock
When one heart strays
Another one will follow
Ask for forgiveness today
Not tomorrow
Then the three shall be
Reunited for eternity

There Is A Rainbow

In the clouds
There is rain
Behind them though
There are rays
Rays of hope and happiness
Silver linings they are called
It is more than that, you see
There is a rainbow
Up there you can see
That is His promise to you and me
There is a beginning to all
And at the end
His grace will fall
There is a rainbow
For each of us to have
Given to us
For our very own
Though we may never touch
The stream of colors
That pass over head
We are sure of a promise
That was given from a Man who once
Was dead
A promise of life ever lasting
And promises made
That are never ever broken
If there ever is a doubt
Just look up and see
Between us there is a rainbow
There is a promise
Given to you and me

There Once Was A Man

There once was a man
Who I couldn't help but know
The road He once traveled
I had yet to go
Though we are from different places
Times were not that different
Because we felt
With the same heart
He came from far away
And I stayed right here
To see His face is to know
The glory
And the magic
That will soon take place
To dream of far away lands and seas
To pick up and follow
Wherever He leads
To know His love
Is just an honor
For I am a lowly servant
That is if He'll have me
I'll do as He says
Speak when told so
You know this Man
Same as me...I know this to be true
For He is the Lord our Savior
And the heart that beats within me
Also beats within you

There Was A Gap

There was a gap
Between us and Heaven
That gap was closed
By Christ on the cross
Just ask for Him by name
And you won't be lost

There was a gap
Between Him and me
That gap was closed
By a prayer answered

There was a gap
Within my heart
But now it is full
Of the blood that won't part

There was a gap
Within your heart
But now it is healed
With a prayer fulfilled

There was a gap
Between us and Christ
Put there by satan
But now the gap
Is closing fast
Because with Christ
There is a love
That will last

Thank You, Lord,
For Standing In The Gap

Those Eyes

Those eyes see
Without judgment
Those eyes speak
Without condemning
Those eyes make a point
Without words
Those eyes dance
Without music
Those eyes know
But stay quiet
Those eyes seek
Without being lost
Those eyes love
Without hate
Those eyes feel pain
Without being noticed
Those eyes cry a sorrow for sinners
Without having sinned
Those eyes laugh
With the beat of a heart in love
Those eyes belong to the Father
Can we see through....
Those Eyes?

Too Many Times

I know You can see me
From that far away
You just follow Your heart
Letting it lead the way
Calling my name-Is easy to do
But what's even harder
Is me calling for You
There is a bond
A direct phone line
No operator need
The bill was paid
Too many times
I've hit my knees
For you and for situations
I know we'll get through

Too many times
I've asked the same things
You've said the same answers
With all of Your heart
You've shown me You care
There is a love
You're willing to share
If I were to ask You
If loving me is a crime
You'd probably say
Ask away
There will never be
TOO MANY TIMES

Touched By A Poem

I heard a poem
Not one my own
But from a man
Who dared let
His heart be shown
With each word read
I felt his heart beat
These words were true
To my heart
And not my head
There was a love
Crocheted within each letter
From one man
To another
A bond built in an instant
Never to be severed
A Godly bond
Nourished by God's love
And grace
A powerful bond
Build at His pace

Under The Wings Of Angels

Car is packed
Goodbyes are said
The light
Is no longer red

Dear Lord hear this prayer:

SEND A LEGION OF ANGELS
BEFORE HIM NOW
DON'T LET SATAN
SHUT HIM DOWN
SET AN ANGEL
UPON HIS CAR
LIFT HIM UP
GIVE HIM THE STRENGTH
TO GO FAR

Beneath the wings of angels
His travel will be guarded
Thanks for his loving heart
Be with him 'til the end
As You were from the start

Voices

When you think
You're all alone
The voices come to call
Which ones should you listen to?
You can't listen to them all
Voices of darkness
May be the flood
Trying to take you
From beneath the Blood
Clawing at your brain
Taking claim to your soul
JESUS, come in and stay
Satan GO AWAY!
Voices of the Light
Come in peace and reassurance
Love, Peace and Kindness
Are just to name a few
If you're really
Right with God
You'll know what to do
Take time
To be with the Father
Get with Him in the Word
Get on your knees
In silent prayer
You'll know the voice you heard

We Shall Be His

From the womb
He had chosen us
Planned out our lives
And asked us to trust
Little did we know
What He had in store
For the two of us
We want so much
To do His will
I know that this
Is also how you feel
We shall be His
If we do things right
So I guess that means
I'll stay up all night
When we talk
We talk things out
Between the three of us
Jesus
You and I
I thought that maybe
You might think I'm mad
It's not true
I thank God for the brother
I've found in you

We Share More Than A Name

There is a three-hour
Time difference
Between here and there
But because of the net
The Bible we share
It is cheaper than calls
Across the states
And quick, with no waits
But when the computer goes down
And the Net's not around
The Bible we pick up
And our rears hit the ground
We should study alone
As much as together
You are there
Any time...wherever
Though I wish to see Del's *smiles* again
I think I can understand
For each time I send
A poem through the E-mail
The computer shuts down
And I murmur 'Oh h...'
Then it dawns on me
What You're trying to say
'Go be with your family, LP...
Del you will again see.'
So...I guess it is safe to say
That Del's prayer was my own
In a funny sort of way
I get the point
I hear what You're saying...
'Get off this computer
The family is waiting.'
Yes, Father, I hear You

What More Can I Say?

I wanted to write more
Than space would allow for
On the inside of a book
Wouldn't you know
Here I go
Doing that poetry thing
I think it's more
Than being blessed
I'm hooked
From the day that we met
And I left the ground
I wondered how
Your voice would sound
On the net
I now see
The words I see
Now, that we've talked
We're closer
You and me
Growing more like family
Each and every day

God had this planned
From our birth days
I cannot wait to see your face
When our kids are running
All over the place
We'll laugh and we'll pray
Thanking God for the day
Our wives will talk
And become best friends
We shall be buddies
The prayers will never end
Time will tell
When that day will come
We will shake hands in the flesh
You'll see
But for now
Over the net our friendship's to be
Computers are quick
That is so true
But the screen can't take the place
Of a smile from you

What Next?

Dear Lord
Your face we seek
Each day of the week
Today Del's Net server went down
Then our knees bent
Faces to the ground
Bible studies are fun
From across the Net
But with our own families
Into the Bible we can't get
I pray this prayer
To know what's right
Give us the knowledge
To stay in Your sight
When should we meet?
When our wives are asleep?
When the children are at play?
Will we see the Blue Letter Bible today?
O Father God, Are You there?

I am
Take care of the families
Then pull in the chairs
The Blue Letter Bible
Is something to share
If you seek Me first
And meet your family's needs right
Then you can study together
Day and night
Be patient my sons
Stop and listen and you'll hear
I will give you
An answer to prayer

When I Think Of You

My heart pounds
When I think of you
Does Yours do the same
When You think of me too?
I know You are there
I see Your face
Wherever I turn
The passion burns
When I think of You
I call out Your name
Soft and low
Do You hear me?
Does Your heart know?
When I think of You
What more can I do?
I pray every day
With every step along the way
Will You answer
When I call
Are You just visiting
Or here to stay?
When I think of You
The love goes deep
Lord, I ask of You
Is this a passion
I can keep?

Which Comes First?

There are times when we are down
When we think He's not around
So little is time
On earth as we know
But where does most
Of our time go?
A little to the family
A little to Him
A little to the Net scene
How do we do it
So it is okay?
The Master is He
Taking priority over all
The family is next
So the strength won't fall
Friends come last
It is true
You'll see
When you want a Bible study
If you can, call on me
I am still praying
For an answer to your prayer
But look in your heart
The answer is there

Why Do You Care?

Why do You care
So much about us?

The ones who love You
Hurt You
And those who are lost
Search for You

We sin every day
Sometimes so much
We want to turn
And go away

No, not You
You stand there knocking at the door
Wondering if we'll hear you
But what are we supposed to do?

You are sinless
We are all sin
We ask for forgiveness
And try to go right again
But the sin and guilt
Crawl in at night
We give in and lose the fight
Why do You care for us?

Why Me?

There is this pull
I feel on my life
I feel like a rubber band
In a tug-a-war
Between righteousness
And sin
The pulling is at my heart
To which do I
Give in?
I want to do what is right
But flashes
Flood in at night
I smile when
I hear your voice
My heart really
Has no choice
To see You
In my mind's eye
Makes me want to cry
Reach out and hold me
Lord
Answer me this...
Why me?

Window In My Heart

There in the window
Is a candle burning bright
Hoping it will lead you home
In the dead of night
At times it burns strong
And full of courage
Other times
It flickers closely
To burning out
That is Satan without a doubt
To know that you
Are there for me
Makes the flame burn higher still

But now you are
So far away
Satan's grip is tightening still
I can't break the grip
In which I feel
A prayer Lord God
Satan will never douse out
The flame that burns
On my heart's window sill.

Worrying About You

I've slept just a bit
Ate even less
Now that you're out there
I can't seem to rest
I've cried my eyes swollen
And now they're real sore
I feel like half my heart
Has been torn from it's core
I wish I was with you
This I know is true
Because I can't do ok
When I worry about you
I know you mentioned Arkansas
And here
If the passes were clear
I've hit my knees over and over
And prayed for His forgiveness
For whatever I may have done
But I can't help but realize
The pain in which I feel
I feel I've lost you forever
And it's not really fun

Write It On My Heart

There have been many times
When You've called my name
But I would not hear
You stood there
Writing all that I've done
Down...on Your heart
Even though I've not denied You
I've often turned from You
I'd proclaim to know You
But failed to do
What You asked me to
I've come back
You've taken me in
I left then again
Only to leave You standing there
Again writing everything
Down...on Your heart
The Blood I felt
Had washed me
I now see in 3-D
May I ask a favor?
Can You forgive the wrongs
And write the rights
Down....on my heart?

You Are Lord Of All

You are Lord of all
You are wonderful
You are a gracious loving God
You carry us
Through the darkness
You lead us
Through the day
You speak to us
And to our hearts
In a gentle unique way
You answer all our prayers
When you see the way
I will love You Jesus
Now...
And from beyond the grave

You Jump...I Jump

There will be times
During our walk with Christ
When we won't feel
Like we should
Or even realize
If the ship you're on
Is going down fast
Grab hold of the One
Who makes life last
The current is strong
The water cold
God is waiting
Right there
You jump...I jump
And together in prayer
We'll get pumped
We are to lean
On each other
And not go it alone
So remember this
When your witness is blown
You jump...I jump
You're not alone

You Melt My Heart

You melt my heart
When You speak to me
The gentle touch
Only I can see
Your words of comfort
Encouragement and Love
I can no longer shove
Your arms
I can feel
Squeeze me so tight
Speak to me
Both day and night
You melt my heart
With the word drove home
Or a simple song
Brought to mind
You make me smile
A laughter I can use
There isn't anything
I wouldn't do for You

You're Gonna Love Me

I knew you before we met
You're gonna love me
I thought
For I love you
That you can bet
I saw you speak from your heart
Listening from the start
I could tell
You're gonna love me
I whispered
Softening that hard shell
I watched as the tears came
Then I reached out
When I heard you call my name
You're gonna love me
I repeated gently
With the beat of my heart
Then one night
On bended knee
You closed your eyes
And asked
You're gonna love me?
One day we shall see
The smile on the other's face
And then I will know
You're gonna love me

You're There

You made it there
I'm still here
I prayed last night
That you would be alright
Your sister called
And told me the news
Now I can start
Getting out of the blues
I cried so hard
My heart ached so
Because I didn't
Want you to go
But now you're there
And you're okay
Give me a call
When you think you can
So that we may stay strong
And keep Satan
From doing wrong
Within this bond
There's a weakened link
If we can't fix it
Satan will change
The way we think
Let's not let that happen

Your Attention, Please

When Your voice
Isn't enough
Things happen
Some good
Some bad
Your Attention, Please
From whispers
To ice storms
Do we listen?
Can we hear?
Your Attention, Please
Simple hugs
To life changing news
Do we listen
When You hear our prayers?
Your Attention, Please
Stuck in a house
For days on end
Where does the fellowship begin?
From Blue Letter Bible on the Internet
To no power at all
Do we hear Your call?
Your Attention, Please
When temper takes over
Or when we're lost and thinking "Geeze"
Do we feel the tug of a heart string
Your Attention, Please

Your Heart Within Me

If my heart
Should skip a beat
Yours beats
In its place
So that I
Won't feel defeat
Or seek another's face
I have to see more
Feel more
Open heaven's gate
And let Your Spirit pour
I gotta be closer
Than ever before
Take me Father
Into Your warm embrace
Love me
As no one else can
Your heart within me
24/7/365
Let me sing and rejoice
Dance and give thanks
That I am alive

Corner's Bend

From the start
Christ got my heart
He blessed me
A special way
In a friend
That will stay
I walk a mile
With Christ in front
The way is straight for now
But the corner is ahead
Will you be there?
I'll reach it
Before you at times
But may I see you
On the other side
Should I turn that corner's bend?
There you are my friend
Christ blesses me again
He stays above
And in front
With you behind watching
I'm safe on all accounts
There will always be a friend
At the corner's bend

Healed In His Eyes

Tonight I was told
As the Spirit took hold
The power of His love
Be shown
I am healed in His eyes
No handicap here
"I have a handicap
It doesn't have me"
I used to say
But now that phrase
Has gone away
For with Christ
There's nothing to fear
My walk is my testimony
For others to see
If they look with His eyes
The legs aren't there
Just Christ within me

Hands To Heaven

Each night
I wonder why
God gave me these hands
They are used for many things
But what they are meant for
If I don't remember to do that
Will God be sore?
My hands are used for loving
The people in my life
Tickling my daughter
And holding my wife
But when I'm alone
And no one is around
Where in the world
Can my hands be found
My knees bend
My face to the floor
My hands become folded
Praising Him
All the more
My hands are to heaven
More now than not
For if it wasn't for Jesus' love
This Life would be shot
So for Christ I will stand
With my feet on the ground
But my hands are forever...Heavenbound

God Pleaser

The change came
Just today
The old me
Was washed away
His blood covered
For a name He called
God pleaser He said
To my confused head
Don't be a man pleaser
       But a God pleaser

Friends Forever

He has a chain
He wears around his neck
A 3-D cross stands out
From the pendant
Friends forever is written
Across the top
When I saw this - Of him I thought
Miles separate us at this time
But with the pendant
I will never leave his mind
This person I talk of
Is special you see
He's my brother
The other half of the pendant
Belongs to me
There is a hollow cut out
Shaped like a cross
If placed together
The pendants would fit
Though worn separately
There is no love loss
Thank God for such a person
I will never forget

Cross Of Diamonds
Band Of Gold

Six diamonds
A band of gold
On the finger
Within my heart's hold
To Him I am a servant
To her I am a Husband
This ring says it all
A wedding ring
It is called
Placed on my finger
A reminder of much
To praise Him
And love her
With a hug or a touch
To them
I should be loyal
I should never
Let them down
With this band
I did wed
This is a blessed marriage
With Christ at the head

Fellow Poet

Bob Carpenter
Were his given names
Plane flying and poetry
Were his games
He wrote a book
Of words that rhyme
Each time I read it
It gets me every time
I laugh I cry
Makes me want to fly
He wrote notes
To his wife, Bea
Everything in the book
Touched even me
From the start
To the end
I felt Bob was my friend
I'm just sorry
I didn't meet him
Before Christ took him home
But I have his legacy
To my kids
I'll make Bob known

Dove Among Roses

It isn't that often
When you see a miracle
To see a child of God
Searching for answers
In a patch full of thorns
Without getting a scratch
She must move
With the grace of a dove
Finding only God's love
Among the roses

Don't lose sight
Of the One
Who can make things right

Never The Same

We speak less now
Than we did before
But I still love you
With His love
That is for sure
A phone call
A letter
Even a beep
Will do just fine
You are always on my mind
Thank God
I have a brother
I can trust with my heart
God's love is within us
That is how we got our start
When we meet face to face
That day will be grand
Together we will praise Him
For all that He has done
Together For Him
We shall stand
Friends we were
Brothers in Christ we became
Thanks to Him
We are never to be the same

My Brother's Cross Pendant

Around my neck
A pendant hangs
A cross
The object
A bond formed
Satan tries
To bust the ties
But this chain
Cannot be broken
I'll not let
Satan take hold
My relationship
With Christ and my brother
Are stronger than gold
Until my death
This pendant I'll wear
At that time
My pendant
Then becomes his
Thank you God
For the pendants we share

Make War On The Floor

He knelt behind me
Just last night
Asking if I'd give my all
Praying I would
Give up the fight
Listen closely
Hear His call
Hands on my shoulders
I felt His touch
Wanting to love Him
Oh so much
I felt the tears
Begin to fall
Step by step
He'll lead the way
Baby steps come after the crawl
Should we stumble
And scrape our knees
Listen closely to His pleas
In the closet
Behind closed doors
Christ gave birth to warriors
We can only
Win the war
If we only
Hit the floor

Man To Man - Brother To Brother

Man to man
Brother to brother
Jesus brought us
To each other
In different states
We live
Looking up
From different shores
We are called
To praise Him
And lift Him higher
Than before

His gifts He will give
If for Him we will live
Man to man
Brother to brother
We are called to help each other
If we stand together
We can overcome all
If we stand alone
We will fall
Stand firm in your faith
Satan will attack
Saying nothing but lies
Believe me, Satan tries
Reach for the Father
Who gave us our start
Remember...
He is the One who
Deserves your heart

Lines Of Communication

To stay strong with Christ
We have to pray
Read the Word
And talk with Him
Even though we cannot see Him
If we do our part
He will make Himself known
Keep the faith
Trust Him

The Lines Of Communication

The same is true
For me and you
In order to stay strong
When life pulls us along
We must talk
I understand that time is limited
For that, I am sorry,
There's nothing I can do
I try my best to keep from crying
When I know that Satan
Is at work lying
God builds me up
So the lies can't take hold
Talking with you my brother
Keeps the friendship hot
It will not go cold

In Her Eyes

Just last night
For her I prayed
Then I got
A big surprise
I saw Satan
In her eyes
The punches flew
Words were said
I received a concussion
To the head
Jesus I prayed
When Sis left
Free her soul
From Satan's hold
To You Lord
My sister I lift
Help me to stay bold

Listen Up
You'll Hear My Heart

"THE HEART OF A MAN" told of a roller coaster ride that we, as humans, may get on at some point in our lives. If you've read it, you may have cried, laughed, praised the Lord and sighed. I'm sorry for mixing your emotions up. Will you forgive me?

"SECOND CHANCE: Taking the Next Step in Love," was just that. A step God gave guidance to and blessed dearly. Knowing one another as He sees us, was one of the biggest lessons taught in writing that book. I wasn't sure if I had it in me, but God…had it in Him. I was just the messenger…

"WE SHALL BE HIS" was definitely written on my heart. I made new friends and my family grew. God showed me that if I let Him rule over everything in my life, He will perform His promises to me…and to you as well. The biggest lesson learned while writing this book was knowing that walking with Christ isn't hard at all. The hard part is the act of walking the line between carnal knowledge and Holy Sanctifying Blood. WOW! What a concept.

Walk by faith, not sight. Believe His Will shall be done in you…and then you truly will be set free…

May His grace be with you…and His blood wash you. Remember, All things happen…IN HIS TIME.

Book Four

In His Time
With every beat of a poem, He knows
my heart

Foreword

There are many people in the world who
enjoy writing, some more talented than
others. It takes a special and unique
ability to finalize a poem or story
and get it written in a way for others to
enjoy. You are one of those with
this special ability as evidenced by your
work.

"In His Time" will help you remember the
great love that is given to each one
of us on a daily basis. Not the love from
our friends and family, but the
love that comes from our Savior, Jesus
Christ. Read this book with an open
heart and mind and you will be able to
enjoy each poem as it passes through
your thoughts.

Once again, David, you have succeeded in
putting together a great work.

God be with you,
Steven P. Miskimens - Author

Book Four

Table of Contents

i

Please Jesus, Rain On Me

You are the living water
You are the living God
You are the Redeemer
Shall we ever walk away?
What more would that say?
We want to love You always
We want to learn Your ways

Satan doesn't like it
When we do that though
For it's not to heaven
He wants us to go

Please Jesus
Rain on me
Take away my sight
Blind me to the darkness
Fill me with the light
Please Jesus
Rain on me

Walk With Me Jesus

Through this dark land
When I look
Are You holding my hand?
Walk with me Jesus
When shadows play
Dear Lord
Keep satan away
When times seem rough
And all looks doomed
Walk with me Jesus
I can't get enough
I'm always alone
Won't you walk with me?
"My child, trust Me.
I will carry you."

Our Journey

In the clouds
He sits and waits
Behind the giant
Pearly Gates
In the Book
He looks to see
For the name
That does say me
Though a sinner
I know I am
In my heart
He has a plan
A mapped-out life
He's given me
He died on the cross
To set me free
Though I should ever
Walk away
In my ears
I'll hear Him say
"Come to Me
Kneel and pray"
Life is more
Than a name in a Book
Seek His face
You'll get the look
Judgment Day
Will come as planned
Then before Him
We will stand
All our deeds
Will be said and done
We will have won

For My Broken Heart

You are near
O Lord
For my broken heart
Cries out
Reach out
O Lord
Let me feel Your touch
I have no need
To want for much
For all I have
You gave to me
Love can cure
A torn heart
Tears are hot
Falling down my face
I seek You
O Lord
In Your Holy place
There is a reason for all
And in Your time
That time will be right
My broken heart is listening
For Your call

His Name Is Joshua David

A child is born
Given a name
Picked from the Bible
Joshua David
That's the one
In his life
Christ's will be done
Strong and courageous
This boy will be
But his birth daddy
He won't see
His Heavenly Father though
Will see this child grow
Where is this child now?
Daddy doesn't know

I cried the day he was born
The day I left
My heart was torn
To my son
I give my love
Joshua David's life I lift
To our Father's care

I Left You At The Altar

I worry too much
This I cannot help
You are a part of my life
But not as important
As Christ
Just ask my wife
The wedge that was formed
Between you and I
Has left me in a whirlwind
Of tears and confusion
I left you at the altar...
No more worries
This I will try
For God has you now
Satan will attack
From both ends
To see if he can destroy
A friendship made with God's control
I left you at the altar...
Now I'll just pray

My Heart Goes On

Asking Him in
Was just the start
Filling me up with gladness
Pumping my heart with love
My heart goes on

Asking Him for guidance
The day we met
Made the bond strong
And is something I won't forget
My heart goes on
Thanks to the friendship
We've formed

Serving Him
As we both do
Living in His love
Is one thing
We both share

As long as He
Is a part of our hearts
Our hearts will go on

Laughter And Salvation

Laughter comes from nowhere
Out loud it sings
A smile cracks my face
Doubt has left no trace
It is the Holy Ghost
You've given to me
Lord, it is You
Who has set me free
Tears fall like rain
More often than not
But it is Your joy
I have got
The joy of salvation
And the knowledge
Of where I belong
Makes me want to
Sing a new song

Prodigal Friend

I think of him always
This best friend of mine
I pray for him
And cry
We talk non-stop from the start
From the mind
And from the heart
Now we speak not
Not even a word
A bond from Christ
Was given
A brother, I feel
Was taken
I pray daily
Hour on end
Lord
I lift him up to you
Restore what has gone
Between me
And my prodigal friend

In Prayer I Believe

Lord-

I see your pictures
All the time
Silent prayers
Rise from mind
Idleness
Satan will not find
Your glory rings out
In all situations
Praises I sing
In prayer
I believe
With You, O Father
There is nothing
I cannot achieve
Honor be to You
O my Heavenly Dad
In serving You
I will be eternally glad

Let Me Praise The Lord

Let me praise the Lord
For the victory
Death is no longer
At my own hand
For the demon
Was banished from me
In Jesus' name
I gave the command
Laughter and song
Replaced where
Sorrow once belonged
To shout His name
And lift it high
Is what I will do
In loving thanks to you

Good Seed

The power of love
A rose in bloom
Stay in His presence
Away from gloom
Clap your hands
Join the song
Feel the warmth
Of the Son
Give rot to the Word
Grow as it feeds
Spread a good seed
Aim for the sky
Call out His name
He will meet you
If even you try

Heavenly Battle

Praise the Lord!
Praise the Lord!
Praise Jesus,
Forever more.

Rock the skies,
Hear the heavens roar!
Go to battle...
Hit the floor.
Yell out loud!
Give the cry!
Send satan home.
Block his every try...
Pray, warriors, pray!
Closer comes the day.

Spirit world rolls,
With Holy thunder...
It is the Holy Ghost coverage,
We are under!
The enemy shall flee,
When we hit our knees.
Chase the father of lies,
Away from here.
Then give out,
The victory cheer!

Welcome

With all due respect
I write this prayer for you
 I don't know
What else to do
I'll lay low
For a while my friend
So as not to bother you
The floor shall be my bed
As the prayers leave my head
I'm not sure
What went wrong
You say satan isn't the cause
I believe he is to blame
Christian friends
May go their ways
But to turn on friends
Isn't Christ's way
I'll pray and pray
Taking hold of the vision
I saw the other day
When you are ready
My door is always open
Don't worry or fret
You know what I'll say
"Welcome"

Let's Go

Let's go! Let's go!
Let's go for Jesus!
Clap your hands,
And shout!

Let's go! Let's go!
Let's go for Jesus!
Give Him the praise,
For the things He's done.
Give Him praise,
The victory is won.
Raise your hands!
Call His name!
You will never be the same!
Move your feet,
And dance.

Let's go! Let's go!
Let's go for Jesus!
The power,
Is in the O Mighty!
Satan,
You haven't got a chance!

Many Are His Gifts

Many are His gifts
To us He gives
His death He gave
For the Godly lives
We live
Strangers we once saw
Are the friends
We now know
A common bond we share
The Lord Jesus
Is here
Rejoice in the laughter
Sing songs
Of the Most High
He's waiting to hear
Your heart's cry
Look, touch, smile
Plant a seed
Give glory to God
That seed will grow
Many are His gifts
We shall soon know

In The Night, Shall You Come, O Lord

In the night, shall You come, O Lord
I rejoice with song
That You are my Savior
Leader of my life
In the night, shall You come, O Lord
I give Thee thanks
For my children
And my wife
In the night, shall You come, O Lord
I pray to You, my God
Then we will be ready
In the night, shall You come, O Lord
I praise Thee
With all my heart
For the layers of love
And the great many gifts
You've given from above
In the night, shall You come, O Lord
I ask Thee
Continue to guide my steps
And my soul feed
Your Word
I want to know
Look upon me, Lord
Let the seed grow

Little Fingers That Move

Thank You Father
For those tiny hands
The ones that clap
And sway in the air
The little fingers that move
About the keys
Releasing sounds
She knows not
O Lord
Look at the smile upon her face
As music fills this place
A home once quiet and empty
Now is known as God's place
The keys I pray
One day she'll learn
Time will tell
As she plays on
O Lord
Bless the little fingers that move
So she may continue to play
A sound so pleasing to You

Candlelight

Last night I saw
Your candlelight
The peace felt right

Newlyweds by right
Shown with brightness
In the night
From them music flowed
A worship to You
So well known
Mighty warriors for Your cause
A love for You
In a soft gentle pause
A glance at each other
A love so clear
Thankful to You Father
For the time they share
Giving You their all
Wanting to go
Wherever You lead
Waiting to hear
Your devine call

Silent Yet Ready

I saw You
O God
In his eyes last night
Friendly to all
Willing to share
Forever grateful
You are there
Somewhere out there
A love looks for him
This, Lord, You well know
A love he waits
For You to bring
His season is upon him
That word
The pastor prayed
A smile this man gave
This silent man
Ready for You Lord
He will stand

Little Prayer

As I lay in bed
Aching and sweaty with fever
My little girl plays
As though I'm a toy
Jumps on the bed
Head-butts to the head
Smacks to the ear
With a wet washcloth
Her laughter rings out
Can't stay mad at her
Takes my pillows
Piles them high
Sits on them
With book in hand
She reads to her Daddy
Or tries to anyway
Then out of the blue
She takes my hand
Closes her eyes
And jabbers away
I think she speaks
And prays in tongues
More than baby talk
He hears the prayers
Of the little ones
This is one Dad
Who is glad of that

William Charles Turns Seven
(11-10-99)

Wow! I can hardly believe it
You turn seven today
Boy, have the years blown away
The last time I saw you
Three months was the age
Kicking and screaming
Inside a playpen
As though you were locked in a cage
I wish I could have been
A better Daddy to you
I don't know where you are
Or what else to do
I pray every day
That you are okay
And hope that we
Will see each other
As friends
If not as father and son
One day
I bet you have grown
Into a bright young boy
Wanting the car keys
And not the toy
I hope that your day
Is full of fun and play
God bless you, William Charles
On your seventh birthday

What If This Happened To Him?

If Joseph had said "No"
To Mary's unborn baby
Where would we go

A child grew within her
A life to live one day
But because of someone's uncertainty
His life was wiped away
"No more children"
The child's Daddy said

A vacuum to the head
Mommy cries
In utter confusion
Daddy is relieved
One less mouth to feed

It may have been
An unwanted child
But it was a child of God's
His plan within that seed
Don't ever fret
If an unwanted bundle comes
It's just another child
Covered in Christ's love

With Him, Without Him

Within me
Flows the River of Life
That which is He

With Him
The Lord my God
I am a warrior of prayer
Making steps
As a steadfast believer
As long as He lives
My heart and soul
To Him I give

Without Him
I would be
A lump of clay
Alone and weary
A target for the world
A victim, its prey

Crossing The Jordan

The passion flows
From within me
It's the muddy Jordan river?
Crystal clear water?
Miracles we shall see

The power of His love
Is like no other
Find your place
With His grace
Provisions we must make
Preparing for the journey
We must take
There, ahead, a river
We must cross
Without Him
We will be lost
Take coverage
Step out in faith
Cross that river
Then we'll see
Just how caring God can be

In Remembrance Of Her

She's gone now
O Lord
You've taken her home
For that we give You praise
She fought the good fight
She taught what was right
She believed in You
O Lord
Her faith was enduring
Her trust in You
Never ending
Her dream was salvation
Salvation for all
In remembrance of
Our dearly departed friend
Anita L. Rustman
O Lord
We shall find the hearts
And lead them to Your call

She Is

She is the love of my life
Who is this I speak of?
Surely you can see
My wife
The better half of me
For three years now
We've been as one
Brought together
By God's only Son
Satan has tried
To untie the knot
But we prayed over his lie
And he could not
Joy fills my heart
Whenever she smiles
Her laughter rings out
When we conquer the trials
She makes my heart flutter
When we kiss
Thank You Lord
For my Mrs.

Star Light

One hand
The stars
Tiny souls
Which home is right
One toss
Across the universe
Gifts are given
What shall they be?
Enter into the Holy Ghost realm
Bring forth His children
Then we shall see

Puzzle Dust

From a box
Puzzle pieces are removed
Placed together
A picture
A band for the Lord is formed
In the box dust remained
From the band
Glory He has gained
Talent no doubt
As music is played out
As the members shout
To the Lord above
Thanks be to Him
For the gifts of
Puzzle dust

From swollen eyes
Tears set free
Here I am
On bended knee
I pray a prayer
Of protection I say
"Please Father God
Don't take this baby away
We've asked for so long
A child to be conceived"
Now, within my wife
Is planted a seed…

Gone is the child
From her within
Not born to this earth
But in heaven
Add one
It saddens us
To see it so
Father, You know what's best
This we know

Look At Me

O Father
I pray
Look at me
Tell me
What You see

What I do
Isn't always right
I ask You, Father
Look at me
Give me insight

Give me strength
When I need it most
Help me
Not to rant or boast

Help me
To welcome the changes
When, You Father
Look at me

Change My Heart

Change my heart
My Lord
My Savior
Give me calmness
In times of stress
Let us look
Within each other
And see the best

Change my heart
To be like You
Guide my steps
In all I do

May my heart sing
The praises of Your name
Change my heart
May I never be the same

Night and day
I seek and pray
Help me to be
All that You ask
Set my heart on the future
Not on the past

O Father, Mighty Father

Your power is great
Your power strong
I want to love You
My whole life long
Teach me Lord
To live for You
Give me the desire
To do what You want me to
Let Your grace and joy
Fill this ol' boy
Give me everything
You want me to have
Teach me
O Father, Mighty Father
To serve Thee

Seed Of Love

When you wake up
In the morning
Sow a seed of love
Go give someone
A great BIG bear hug

Jesus loves you!

Reflection In The Ripples

Within the ripples
Of the river
Who do I see?

Christ?
Or just the old me?
Is this an illusion
Or really true
Dear God
What can I do?
I know He is my Savior
I know He's in my heart
But sometimes I feel
I've lost it all
And I'm back at the start
I know that I'm forgiven
Yet I lift this prayer to You
When I look within the ripples
The reflection I want to see
Is You

Sunset-Sonrise

Sunset
Death in the world
Sonrise
Eternal life

Sinner's Admission

With our hearts
We believe
With our mouths
We confess
Will You, Lord
Do the rest?
Sinners we admit to be
Salvation we accept
Will You, Lord
Set us free?

Sinner's Poem

Let Jesus
Hear the cry
Or in darkness
You will die…

You died, Lord Jesus
You paid the price
I'm a sinner
I'll not deny
Come into my life
Take control
From satan's hand
I'm letting go
Take the sins from me
Set me free

His Moment

Hands in front
Fingers inner laced
Eyelids down
Tears cried
Prayers embraced
Prayers for the sinners
Prayers for the lost
Prayers for their salvation
My life will it cost?
Father, take this cup from Me
Lest I drink it all
Your will be done
For their souls You call
I must go to the cross
Free Your people from darkness
Bring home the lost

Heart Start

I love You, Father
With all my heart
Please, Lord
Put an end
To the darkness
And let the Light start

More Precious Than Gold

You are a treasure
In the eyes of God
You have more worth
Than you ever thought

Rubies and diamonds
Sapphires and pearls too
Are priceless in the sight of God
But the do NOT compare to you

Sometimes when you feel down
You may think you aren't of value
Just remember that
God has more love
And He wants to give it to you

Don't give up your dreams
Although it may be true
That you've already done that
But God's going to see them through

So you keep on believing
And know that you were told
That God loves you so much
Because you are more precious than gold

PTL

Praise the Lord
For the life He gave
So I could live
The life He made

Praise the Lord
For all He's done
The battle over darkness
Has been won

Praise the Lord
For the love He shows
Within me
His Holy Spirit grows

Little Eyes

Those little eyes
I see
For God's help
They plead
Trying hard to obey
Their mom's every say
Outside they play
To stay out of the way

Jesus I ask
On their behalf
Set their family
In a place
Where they all
May seek Your face
I know You see
Those little eyes
Please Lord answer
The silent cries

Let Us

Let us give
Not take
Let us love
Not hate
Let us shout
Not pout
Let us rejoice
Not stifle our voice
Let us go up
Not down
Let us smile
Not frown
Is Jesus calling you?
He's waiting
Let us bring Him home
Not cast away
Invite Him into your heart
That is where to start

Fire Fall

Lord, I give You the praise
For moving into this place
Pierce the hearts within
Thirst and hunger
For the fire You have
Spirit and passion fall
On those who call
Give us the anointing
You want us to have
Mighty God
Open the heavens
And let the fire fall
Praises rise up
Blessings come down
Let the fire fall, Lord
Hear our hearts sound

Bramble

Let me be above all
Seek refuge beneath my wings
I will keep you safe
Give you power
Hide in my authority
Shhh...
I have nothing to give
No substance
By which I live
I am a bramble bush
A shell am I
Lift me up
And within my shadow
You can hide
Shhh...
Yet if you seek the truth
You'll know that I lie

When All Is Said And Done

Will I be the one
He calls forward with a smile?
Or the one
Sent away distrusted and vile?
The world is a powerful place
Be not of it
Walk in His grace
Great is the Lord
And the Lord is He
He's still working on me
I pray to the Father
Both day and night
I may not be perfect
Or even do what's right
But...
When all is said and done
I pray it is His smile I see
And not the darkness of night

The Master's Hand

A simple gesture
Fingers laced between each other
Words spoken
A gentle whisper
Warmth and comfort
Firmness for sure
One touch is all it takes
Satan's hold breaks
Illnesses confronted
Cured!!
Healing confirmed
Strength to correct
Softness to love

Eyes And Heart

Eyes full of fight
Heart to know what's right
Eyes dancing with excitement
Heart that hungers
Eyes that search
Heart to accept
Eyes to see what needs to be done
Heart full of love
Eyes asking for more
Heart with an open door
Eyes needing forgiveness
Heart that gives it
Eyes that know the Father
Heart that knows the children
Eyes to follow Jesus
Heart to ask us to follow

Eyes and Heart…
One sees
One feels
Where else should we start?

You Took My Hand

I felt something from within
When my hand you shook
The Spirit spoke
There you stood
I heard His voice again
'Does he know Jesus?
Show him
Tell him
Love him into the kingdom'
Look beyond the stars
For the One who placed them there
I thought as you talked of the night
There is a reason we met
He directs our paths
You didn't know it then
I did
Do you desire to know Him
As He knows you?
We shall meet once more
There will be an open door
I pray my friend
God speaks to you
And in your life
His will you will do

Do You Remember Me?

On this day
I think of you boys
Thirty is just another year older
Turning it
I have no choice

Do you remember me?
Though it was
So long ago
I wonder now
If you even know

The pain I feel inside
Gains with each day
That passes by
Do I even have
The right to ask
Do you remember me?

If I can't be your Daddy
Let me at least be your friend

Does Jesus ask me that question?
DO YOU REMEMBER ME?

He Has A Plan

He has a plan
That we all should understand
But it is for Him to see
I understand His glory
I understand it's for His glory
It was for our salvation
That He went through
All that pain
He walked this road before us
He was tempted
The same as you and I
Though He never gave way
For the thoughts to take Him in
At the cross of Calvary
He gave way
To our sin

I Surrender All

I

Surrender to His love
Under Him I shall be
Remembering Who gave me life
Relying on His strength
Ending life as I knew it
Never to go back
Demanding satan to leave
Encouraging others
Realizing His power

And asking for the knowledge
Learning from it and
Leading others with it

Give It To Him

We spend all our lives
Wandering about
Waiting for Him to move
We say "Yes"
Then we wait
Wait
And wait

Let's do our part
With Christ in our hearts
Move towards Him
In faith
In trust
Give it to Him
Go for God or bust

If you want
To see Him move
Start walking

Where The Men Gather

In a place above
A mountaintop
Where the Spirit of God
Will not be stopped
Learning the lessons
Becoming real men
Godly men
Living the life
We are so within
The power and strength
The knowledge given
Everything received
In places unseen
Glory to the King
Praising God
For all He's done
Focusing on the Holy One
Loving Him with worship and song
Being lifted to a higher level
No longer left to wonder 'why?'
Climbing up as one man
Going down as another
I've climbed that climb
I've reached the top
His teachings begin here
Where the men gather---
At the SUMMIT!

One On One

One on one
Me and the Holy One
Me with the questions
Him with the answers

Holy Ghost coverage
Over us all
With the knowledge gained
Satan will fall

Music and worship
Fill this place
As we seek
His loving face

Each person's life
Will surely change
Made clear and white
No longer stained

Praise and glory
Are His to be had
His grace is upon us
For this we are glad

Real Men

Desiring the Word
Reading the Word
Knowing the Word
Praying
Praying hard
Praying for the church
The saints
And His will to be done
Walking in His will
Standing for the kingdom
Striving for the kingdom
He's looking for real men
Are you one?
Are you serving God?
Real men
Let God take control!

O Lord

Use me O Lord
For I want to be used
Your will O Lord
Sets within me
Set it free
Take me O Lord
To another level
I want to leave 'me' behind
To be with You
Tell me O Lord
What it is I need to do
Guide me O Lord
In Your steps
I want to walk
Replace my tongue O Lord
Like You I want to speak
Carry me O Lord
My strength is drained
I cannot walk alone
Fill me O Lord
With the Holy Spirit
From You O Lord
I'll receive
To my knees I fall O Lord
I surrender all

That Day

Like paper it tore
For hell I was headed
For sure
Muscles cut
Blood poured free
I wanted to end life
As it was known to me
Darkness arrived
On closed eyelids
Talking to stay conscious
I knew it was wrong
This had gone on
Way too long
On the table
Jesus spoke
My awareness awoke
A seven-inch opening I saw
I had listened to the wrong call
Glory be to Jesus
For the life I live today
On Mother's Day 1998
The demon of suicide
Was forever cast away
Praise God!

Bound No More

Smiles on the faces
Tears in their eyes
Truth can be tough
Down with the father of lies

To us be the knowledge
To Him be the glory
End the old book
Start a new story

A shower of blessings
About to be had
Today is His
Rejoice and be glad

A new day
His way
Bound no more
By satan's hand
For the rock of Jesus
As new men we stand

Mountain Top

From the mountain top
We shout
"He is Lord!"
There is no doubt

Wake us up
Deploy us for service
For You we shall strive
Being bold
Not wimpy and nervous

Mountains shall move
Should we say the word
You gave us the power
The instruction we heard

Sunrises and sunsets
Your gifts
For the world to see

Let us take hold of Your wonders
Set the Spirit-man inside us free

The Wall

Which wall are we behind?
The wall of salvation?
The wall of sin?
One is built by the Spirit
The other by the flesh
To which one will we give in?
Christ is in control
His love resides in us
If we walk with Him
And talk with Him
We build a bond
A trust
We learn lessons every day
Not knowing the reasons
But He knows the way
He'll lead us through
Not leave us scattered about

His Words I Hear

The words I hear
As He softly speaks
Touched I am
Tears begin to streak
Gently He wipes
The moisture away

"I gave My life
So in sin
You don't have to stay"

In His eyes
I could see
Concern, truth
And love for me

"Father," I asked
"Why is it so difficult?"

"You, My child
Were destined from birth
To proclaim the Gospel on the earth
How hard is it
To say you believe?
Surely easier, I know
Then to die on a tree"

From This Canyon

Here I am, Lord
At the bottom again
It sure is cold
In this here canyon
Where are You, I wonder?
Can You hear me?
Forgive all I've done?
I know You do, Lord
I'm just confused
Frustrated too
Can I, Lord
Hear from You?
Great is the day
And the joy You give
Can I get closer, Lord
Heavenly Father
In Your shadow
I want to live
Bring me, Lord
Out of this canyon
High above the depressive destruction
Of this place
I want to see, Lord
Your smilin' face!

An Asset To The Company

Working next to the most important
Employer of all
Can be a challenge

What can I bring into the company
To let others know just how important
This work must be

God does not discriminate
And accepts anyone who wants
To do the work of the Father

Ready to work
Willing to pray
Wanting the best for our Savior
Is a requirement for the company

Teamwork's important
Helping hands and a caring heart
Are also needed for the position

God accepts us
We need to be willing
To do the work for our Lord
And be an asset to the company

Because He Lives

Life has never been the same
As it was the day He came
Into my life one blessed day
That day He washed my sins away

God has made me one true friend
From the beginning till the end
He reached His arms out on the cross
To show His love to the lost

Sometimes when I'm weak
I have to watch the words I speak
There isn't anything He doesn't know
When I think how He loves me so

We see His love everywhere
And knowing just how much He cares
Only true life Jesus gives
And it's all because He lives

The Road

There is a road we all must travel
Might be of pavement or gravel
Such as life
Darkness eludes us
Eyes adjusting to the vastness
Of the surroundings
Only to see shadows of gray
If given a chance - a choice
Between night and day
Which would you choose
Or would you stay?
Jesus waits at one end
Arms open
Mouth quiet
Eyes saying it all
Satan at the other
Finger pointing voice echoing
Eyes taunting
What will it take
For you to see
The errors of your ways?
Make the choice
It's your decision
Pavement or gravel?
Jesus or the world?
Think about it
Is Jesus the pavement
Or the gravel?
Which road will you travel?

In memory of Francis Joseph Wagner
1921-1999

Back To The Beginning

From the heart of God
We are destined
In the image of Christ
We are defined
Since birth from the womb
We search for Whom
Has given us our lives
As the seasons change
And years pass by
Some find the answers
Some wonder "Why?"
We all have a beginning
And a part in which to play
If we listen closely
With focused ears
"Are you ready?
Be at peace. Come see the glory.
Laughter is in the coming years."
As humans we shall pass away
Only He knows when and where
So be ready for gosh sake
Who knows when it's there
Into the ground
Covered in dirt we shall be
But life doesn't stop at the grave
For in heaven
Life begins for thee...

In Memory Of Francis Joseph Wagner

I'll walk the streets of gold
His tender hand I'll hold
I'll see the loved ones left behind
And cheer as they meet their goals
Surely they will cry
For I am no longer there
But the memories of my earthly life
We will go on to share
The trumpets sound
That glory song
As through the clouds I'll look on
I may have been an old fart
Who had an attack of the heart
But death cannot stop
This mighty man of God's
Soil has become my blanket
And death warmed me over
But when I died
Christ reached out
And took me to His side
Sin holds me no longer
Now with Him I will walk
About the family we shall talk
Don't cry so much
That I am gone
Or think, "What shall we do?"
My time on earth was done
I've gone back to the beginning
And someday so will you

Summer's Day

The clouds
Cotton above us
The wind
Yet a whisper of love
The sun
Warm kisses from the heart
Falling leaves
Deception pealed away
A single raindrop on a summer's day
Truth be told
Two people together with Him
One
The goal
His will
Not just in another's eyes
But in another's heart
A gift from God
Hand in hand
Walking with each other
No words needed
Everything known
One heart embraces the other
A song sounds
Magic that only they know

True love...

Deep Within Her

Deep within her
I see a passion from him
One that grows stronger
By the day
Filling her whole
In every way

Deep within her
I see a passion for the husband
She calls me
Though there are times
I've lost my way
Firmly she stands
With "I love you" to say

Deep within her
I see a passion
For the child we share
The loving mother
The laughter and hugs
A mother-daughter bond
Nothing will tear

All That Glitters

All that glitters
Isn't silver or gold
But the love of Jesus
Your heart holds

Nor is it fame or fortune
But being right with him
And knowing the peace within

Hold tightly
To what He freely gives
Walk in the warmth of Light
Not in the darkness of sin

Beat Him To The Punch

When times are dark with confusion
And life's not what you want
Satan's gonna hit you
With everything he's got

Emotions flare
Tears flow
You think there's nowhere to go
At some point
You'll be on your knees
Beat him to the punch

Ask Jesus in right there
Break satan's constant hold
Give Jesus full control

Tell satan to take a hike
You want to do what's right
You don't really want to die
Life is a prayer away
Right then and there
Talk with Jesus
He's listening to what you have to say

Beat satan to the punch-accept Jesus' love
today!

Heaven Is For Children

Hell is for satan
And his unholy clan
He tries to wear you down
With unclean thoughts
Or whatever he has found

Grab your Bible
Read it now
Show him where you stand

Satan may use enemies
You may not know you have
To take you out
He'll do whatever he can

You've made the Lord
Ruler of your life
For you there is no doubt

Death may come at any time
You'll stare it in the face
Satan has no time to waste

Give thanks to the Lord
For His will be done
Heaven is for children
Of His you are one

Do You Have Diarrhea?

How much pride do you have
Building up within?
Fearful to scream and shout?
Break out of the bubble
Freak out and explode
The Holy Ghost takes control
Face the fear that's holding you back
Inside there's a wall
Pride is going to fall
Down your leg it will run
Stinky and vile is the pride of life
Feel that feeling on the backside?
Or is it deep inside?
Let loose
Get comfortable with the uncomfortable
Get diarrhea - let go of pride
And see God move

Maple Lane

Today the stone
Was rolled away
Behind these walls
You won't stay
Satan held at bay
The shackles shall break
The cuffs shall melt
As my tears fall upon them
Here I stand watching
As you go beneath the wave
Sin and shame fall loosely
Taking with it the blame
No matter the crime
Redemption is here
No matter the sin
The blood of Jesus
You are standing in
Rejoice all you men
Speak to me, my children
For your Father is listening
My arms are out
Please enter in
Today the stone
Was rolled away
Step up in the Spirit
Your new life begins

Behind These Bars

For years I've watched you come and go
Search for something
But of Me, you didn't know
You are here
For something done wrong
I now have your attention
Teachings shall be taught
Lessons shall be learned
Behind these bars
Your flesh is captive
Yet your mind is free to roam
Give thanks in all situations
For good is made of the bad
Let me in and lead you home
I saw what you did out there
Why do you think you're in here?
Now I have your attention
Satan cannot hold you
Once I have your heart
Read My word
And know My will
Let the inner wounds heal
I've called you - step up
For your souls I've wept
Let the sin go - the old you die
Let me resurrect you behind these bars

Restore The Fire

Deep within
The heart of this man
There's a search going on
Though I know
Where the answers are
I cannot seem
To reach that far
I rejoice when I praise Him
I long to follow Him
At home I'm lost
Totally confused
Wanting to read the Word
Yet lacking the desire
O Lord, restore the fire

Like Birds

Like birds we are
Held captive in a cage
Not placed here by society
But by sin and inner rage
For the sin
This is the consequence
Behind bars we sit
The world outside is distant
For salvation, Lord
We go to the bench
Mighty men of God
We wish to be
Reach into our hearts, Father
Set us free

RPMG

Read the instructions
Pray for wisdom
Memorize the Word
Go and spread the Gospel

Instructions For Men

Learn to teach
Receive to give
Serve to lead
Die to live

Any questions?

Wash In Tears

Wash in His tears
Encased in grace
Know the power within
Walk upright
Away from sin
Lay hands on the ill
Pray in the Spirit
See the vision
Seek Him still

Are You the Man?

Men of God
Read the Word
Learn then teach
Mentor the youth
And for the many lost
You'll step out and reach
Love your family
As Christ loves the church
Care for the children
Pray healing on the hurt
Be strong
Be bold
On bended knee
Let your hands fold

Silence Sounds Aloud

Head bowed
Hands folded
Silence sounds aloud
Love your wife
Like never before
Take her with you
Pray
Open that spiritual door
Step forth
Kneel down
Place yourself
On common ground
Let your silence sound aloud

Give Up Control

To be male
Is by birth
To be man
Is by choice
How do you live your life?
Let's hear you voice
Stand up
For the things of Christ
Are you the man
Or is it your wife?
Take responsibility
Step into the role
Give Christ His right
Give Him control

Heavenly Impressions

Impressions upon the heart
Sent from above
For men to know Christ
And be closer to His love

If Given The Choice

If given the choice
Which would you do?
Help the needy
Or just yourself?

Step out of yourself
For one moment please
What did Christ do
When He started to bleed?

Would He have walked away
From a child with teary eyes?
Would He have left us
To our own pain and lies?

Honor thy mother and father
Feed the hungry
Clothe the naked
Spread the Gospel
That is what He asks of us.

We are not to let another
Go without or ever wonder why

If they want to see Jesus,
Let them see Him in your eyes.

The Rock Is He

Immovably solid yet gentle
Refuge for the weary
Jesus is the rock

Take With You

Take with you
The heart of God
See the blessings arrive
Pray as you go
For those you know
Watch for the dead lives to drop
And the new ones to come alive

Fence Line

Half in - Half out
Wanting the world
Loving Him without a doubt
The fence can hurt
You know what I mean
The sins you do
Have not gone unseen
Repent and know
The true love of Christ
Listen to your Father in Heaven
Wise you will be
Past the shadows of darkness
Freedom you shall see

Confusion

We as humans
Don't always understand
The world is the world
Christ is the Man
His life He gave
For people He didn't know
The kingdom of God
Is a worthy cause
Before we sin
Do we think or pause?
Great is the Lord
The door is He
Ask Him for clarity
Pass the confusion we shall see

Flesh

Lust of the flesh
Often means no rest
Giving into the "feel good"
Not walking away as we should
Is there a medium
Where we can do both
Without having to hang
From a guilt rope?

Red Drops

The color of love is Red
As is the blood
The Lord shed
With each drop He painted
The canvas of our lives white
As a painter with a brush
The boarder that binds us vanish
With every stroke of His love

Let Him create within you
The picture He sees
Will you allow Him
To paint on your canvas with ease?

Beside Me

He stands beside me
When I think not
He calms the fear within
For grace He's got

His protection is great
His love is mighty
As I walk with Him
This man I call Father
Satan cannot hold me

Though my body
May be confined to this world
My mind and soul belong to Him
With my Father beside me

I Cried...He Cried

I cried today
As my child called my name
"I'm sorry," I softly said
As I went to work
"Daddy," she screamed, "No"
Tears began to burn fast
"Lord," I prayed
"Let this day pass"

He cried today
As the lost reject His name
"I'm sorry," He softly said
As the child goes his way
"Daddy," He wished they'd call
Tears began to burn fast
"My child, My child
I watch and I see
You'll be lost without Me"

If He Fudged It...

He could have fudged it up
Having dropped the ball
If He had
Look where we'd be
One and all

Dancing on flames
With only ourselves to blame
That wouldn't be fun
I'd rather walk on clouds
Close to the Son

With Each Step...

With each step...

I ask You, Lord, please enter in
I say, Lord, I love you
With each step...

My faith grows stronger
I'm lost no longer
Satan falls behind
Your love and warmth I find

With each step...

My desire for You shows
My hunger is filled

Though my walk may not be perfect
And certainly not always straight
I know that with each step that is weakened
You Father, become my strength

Walk By Faith...Walk On Water

May my feet
Never touch unholy ground
With each step I take
Your word and heart be known
For it is my name
I hear You holler
May the lost be found
Your voice has sounded
The heart will cry
The old will die
We shall walk by faith
Keeping our eyes on You
We shall walk on water

His Way Made Clear

Tonight was the night
I saw the Light
His glory
His grace
His gifts
Released within me
A power
A flare
The FIRE is there
To heal
To speak
For the glory of God
Thank You Father
For the new me
A firmer Christian
People will see
His WILL made clear
Set fire in me

Heaven's Eyes

Up here I can see down below
I watch to see how they go
Like mice they scurry
Living life in a hurry
Should they ever want to stop
I will be there before they drop
Seeing and knowing all that you do
Tears of joy may fall today
If you decide to come my way
You should hear me laugh and sing
When you do the right thing
Run from Darkness to the Light
Give Me your life
I'll give you mine
When you need Me
I'll be here
Just look into Heaven's eyes

This Way...That Way

In life
I've found
There are struggles
One hand pulling me this way
The other pulling me that way
Emotions forever twisted
Going up
Going sown
Jesus is the Rock
Sing praises to His name
He gave life to the dead
For sins we would shed
We shall never be the same
Take courage in His love
Knowing that from above
Happiness and harmony
Shine down
Whenever you acknowledge
He is around

The Victory Is Ours

The time has come
To sing and praise
For He has released us
From the chains
PRAISE GOD THE ALMIGHTY
Satan plays with minds
If in idle it finds
We start to think
The carnal thoughts
If from God
We get lost
The pain and suffering
Satan gives
Is tossed away
Because God lives
The victory is ours
This is true
He broke the chain
From the past and sin
For everyone...INCLUDING YOU!
Sing praises and dance for hours
In Him
The VICTORY is ours!

Super Hero

You can walk through life
All on your own
Tired and alone
Weary and heavy laden
Give up the burden
Give up the fight
I'll be your super hero
No matter how far you walk
You'll never leave darkness
Unless you find the Light
I'll be your super hero
Give Me the chance
To carry you
Give Me the load
I'll take the steps
That you can't bare
Your super hero
Will always be here
You will have a place to go
Don't turn away
I want to stay
I'm your super hero

Sealed With Tears Of Love

The request was made
With the task in mind
The carpenter chosen
A bed is to be made
The wood picked
The best nails too
This will be hard
For this carpenter to do
Molded to the customer's liking
She knows this isn't easy
Christ be with him
As he begins this project
With each nail placed
Each swing of the hammer
A tear falls
For his Father's strength
The carpenter calls
Tears of love splash
To seal the wood
Per her request
He'll do the best he should
Prayers he says
With each sobbing cry
Thanking Him
For their time together
"She's ready Lord
Take home this wife of mine."

Some I Know Not

He walked in
"The mountain man"
They thought
"Some of you," He said, "I know
Some I know not"
They sat in awe
They sat in fear
"Some of you run
Some draw near
Fill yourselves to overflowing
Don't be a shell
Dance with Him in heaven
Not on the flames of hell
The physical body
You all see
Yet a few
Know the real Me
I've watched you men
Come and go
Among the world's troubles
Follow Me
And freedom you shall see

Drink Deeply

In a time
When people were dying
What are we t o do?
Where are we to go?
We're a thirsty nation
Drying out – Cracking
Living water is near
Why are we running?
What is it we fear?
Christ is the answer
For this dying world
Fill your cup
Fill your soul
Drink deeply
What is given
Drink in the Word
Really start livin'

Mountain Be Moved

There's a point
We all reach
Where pebbles are gathered
Rocks are heaped
Financial stress and relations
Are mountains at best
Speak nicely of someone you hate
Scream and shout
Let the hermit out
Something will happen
Just you wait
Put away normalcy
Break out the unusual
Watch and see
Christ begin to move
Tossing your mountains
Into the sea

That's what happens
When you speak mountainese

Frog Fry

Anger and frustration
Bitterness and strife
It's time for a frog fry
Loose tongues
Bad words slung
Catch those frogs
The pan is hot
Nine lives
The frogs have not
Move away from the boarders
The center in Christ
Clean your mind
Clean your home
Think twice
Before letting your frogs roam

The Nations Cried

Hitler's birthday
Hell broke loose
Shots and screams galore
Panic and terror
Horrific for sure
What was all this for?
No one understands
The only question, "Why?"
Many died
The nations cried
Lives ended – others destroyed
Some stood boldly
In the time of fear
One thing is clear
God saw it all

Is There A Home?

Dirt for a bed
No pillows for the heads
No food to eat
Just bones
No meat
Please God
Help these little ones
No place to call home
Just the streets to roam
Some day the future will be clear
They won't have to live in fear
Where is their next meal?
Where is the water?
To clean the wounds
And help them heal?
For now they make it
With what they have
But Christ will send help
To their land

Let A Child See

Praise and laughter
For all to hear
Songs of great joy
Ring through the air
Dancing, running
Jumping and playing
Energy - Give me more
Thanking the Lord
For all that we have
Taking advantage
Of the simple things
Holding tightly
Not willing to share
Is there anyone out there
Who really cares?
Give what you can
Of yourself if nothing else
Let the child share
Know and see
The grace and love
God blessed upon you and me
Give a child a hug - a kiss
Share the things
The child might miss
Don't be hard hearted
Careless and cruel
Show compassion
Let Christ use you

Shall We Be Consumed

Are we Priests?
Or Kings?
Do we eat from the tree of Life?
Or good and evil?
Are we going up?
Or staying at ground level?
Do we breed rats?
Or kiss frogs?
Are the emergency lights on?
Or have they gone off?
Do we live in the gutter...on the boarder?
Or the center of Christ?
Do we help others?
Or just ourselves?
Do we want normalcy?
Or a revival?
Are our eyes closed?
Or wide open?

Shall we be consumed?

As Long As I Am

Too many times
I wonder just what's there for me
What am I doing?
Where am I going?
Then the Lord
Gently speaks to me

"They are there
Family, friends
The passion for Me
I AM He
And I AM here for you
There is nowhere
You cannot go
And no one
You cannot love
The times are never too many
As long as I AM here

Tears For A Nation

The tears you cry
Are for the nations
The passion you feel
Will explode
My Word
Within you unfolds
The strangers there
Shall see that you care
Travel and trust
The provisions set by Me
Reach out and touch
The hearts not near
Go, My child, into the nations
Let the Gospel
Their ears hear

Comfortable...Uncomfortable

Break free
From that bubble
Don't worry
About the trouble
Move out of yourself
Fear not what may be there
I've made the way clear
Go forth – you have favor with Me
Protection is before you
The dangers subdued
No harm shall come
Share what I say
See the fruit
Souls set free
Let your testimony
Glorify Me

My mouth...Your Words

I try to stay
All to my own
My lips still
Words unknown
My tongue dances
When my lips part
Not hearing
Thoughts from my heart
Slow to speak
For this and strength
For You I seek
Fill my mouth, Father
With Your Words
Joy and praise
Give me, Lord
That just right phrase

Stand In The Gap

On one side is Christ
On the other the world
The angels rejoice in heaven
The demons prowl the earth
Blessings are there
Testimonies to share
Lost souls search
Saved souls pray
We must stand in the gap
For those we cannot reach
His Word we preach
Christ stood there for us
Our turn is now
That space is to be filled
Lest their fate be sealed

Joshua David Turns Eight
(06-22-99)

Oh boy
It's hard to believe
Another years has passed
Between you and me

Many prayers have gone up
For you in the name of love
Though I think of you always
I worry not
Your protection comes from above
And the trust in God I've got
You are eight
What a young man you must be
I'm not there
To give a birthday hug
More than ever
On this day
I send my love
No card was mailed
Since all sent out return
All in all
I pray that on this birthday
The Lord blesses you

Where Are You?
(Joshua and William)

I haven't seen you both
In nearly seven years
Many prayers are said
I believe God hears
I've told your sister about you
But Anita Rose doesn't understand
Why daddy talks of brothers
She never thought she had
Joshua is eight
William is soon to be seven
Anita Rose is nearly three
Because of you all
A father was made of me
Do you know who I am?
Do you remember then?
No letters or pictures
Come my way
I know not where
You are today
I know the day is coming
I trust this much is true
We will meet face to face
There won't be time to waste
I'll say, "I love you"

I See Fruit

Every morning
I'm beginning to see
Fruit from my daughter
She's nearly three

She cries when one of us leaves
That's natural I know
But there are signs
That now show

She says "Amen"
When prayer time is done
She picks up things
With a smile and laugh

Great is the God
We all have

Great Are The Blessings

Great are the blessings we receive
Each day we get small ones
We wait for the big
Trusting in Jesus
For the blessings to give
Blessings can be obvious
Or even unseen
Faith is such as that
Growing stronger by the day
Helping others we meet
From time to time
This is fun
It's a blessing just to give
Increasing the faith
In which we live

One Fine Day

Each day that I live
Is one fine day
I wake with expectation
What will He do today?
Will my attitude stay in check?
My tongue in a knot?
I pray for opportunities
To give blessings away
It may not be much more
Than the words that I say
There are things to be done
Souls to be won
The days are what we make of them
Make them all
One fine day

Day In And Day Out

Happiness and laughter
Great is the joy
Christ is King
Christ is Lord

Day in and day out
Minute by minute
We can walk by faith
His presence is there
Can you feel it?

You choose to do
Day in and day out
Selflessness is a blessing
You'll see
Don't hoard the things
He gives to you
Give away what you can
See what God will do